Blind Bird

KRISTYAN PEREZ

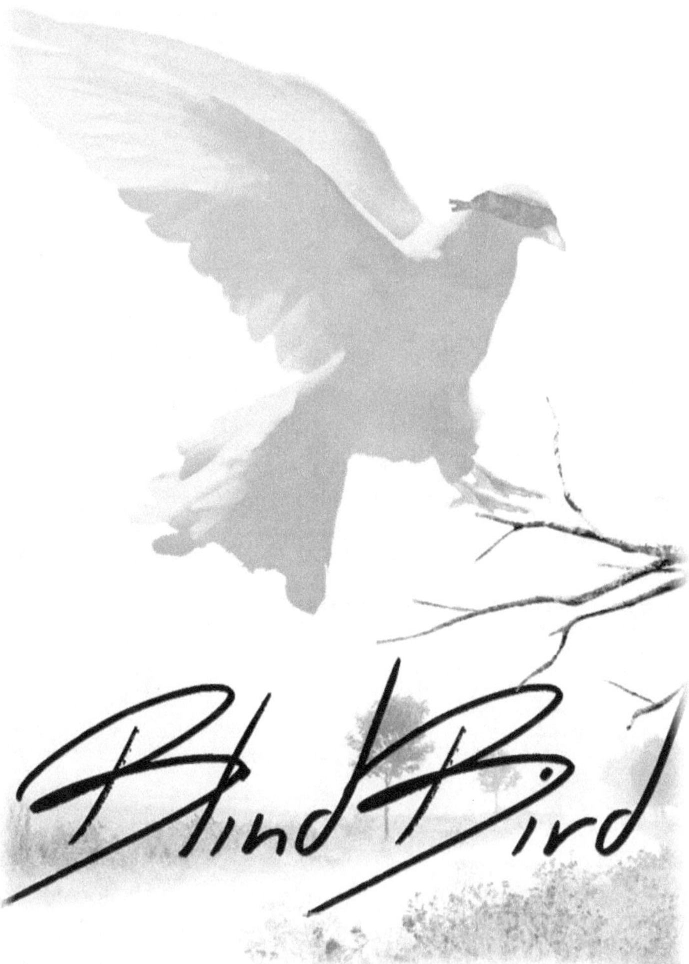

Blind Bird

KRISTYAN PEREZ

Lithonia, GA

© 2021 Kristyan Perez
All rights reserved. No part of this book may be reproduced in any form without permission in writing from the publisher.

Publisher:
MEWE, LLC

ISBN: 978-1-7360565-0-9

Library of Congress Control Number: 2020921391

Disclaimer Statement: I have tried to recreate events, locales and conversations from my memories of them. In order to maintain their anonymity in some instances, I have changed the names of individuals and places; I may have also changed some identifying characteristics and details such as physical properties, occupations and places of residence.

For Worldwide Distribution
Printed in the USA

This book is dedicated to my mother: you are beautiful in all the ways I hope to be.

This book is also dedicated to all women, past and present, and to any woman's child, who has struggled to piece together a life after sexual abuse.

Table of Contents

Prelude ix

Chapter 1 1

Chapter 2 5

Chapter 3 5

Chapter 4 11

Chapter 5 15

Chapter 6 19

Chapter 7 23

Chapter 8 25

Chapter 9 29

Postlude 31

Prelude

In some societies, women gather around in circles telling stories. Women – these maids and masters of all the world, bearers of life – these diamonds, in the beauty and strength of our force, are so commonly overlooked, undercut, ravaged, trampled. For a woman to share her triumphs, is to display all her worth for the glory of God. And to find this glory intact, like a grain of gold obscured by every feature in our path, is everything we could wish for. The ultimate goal of all our wanderings is wisdom.

I've needed this gathering since I was born. There's something to be said about the proximity, the tone, the words, and the summations of gathering and telling. Wisdom in our world today doesn't receive the attention it warrants, but, daughter, sister, it is among the most important of pursuits. When we don't have it, we need to seek it like the water and air we need for life. I'll take my turn now in this circle to impart what I have found and tell you why I rejoice.

I do so, though, with trepidation. The history I will relay is one overwrought with affliction, which my own eyes observed, and my own heart bore. And the most horrifying fact of all is that this is not my story alone, but one shared by so many others on dark nights.

Children the world over are sexually abused by trusted adults – members of their own families. Awful things happen to children in the very cities we believe are safe and functional, under a justice system that chronically fails the innocent. In being written rather than told out loud, and read rather than more heard through ears, the details of my experiences are no less tolerable. But they are the truth and, therefore, bound to be revealed at last.

To write the chronology of any pain is not an easy task. The mind can tell the hand the words to scratch down, but then there's this: the need of the heart to allow, pardon and accept, and to predict what could happen when you give this thing life by writing about it. As if all along, it hasn't already had life! In fact, it was fully alive and growing like some giant predatory weed. The thing is, without being written, it can seem lighter to deal with – cobwebs and dust. To put the words of it down for eyes to see and hands to touch, it feels like giving to a very deadly thing, a thing that could take those roots and regenerate, and grow to new heights. In spite of the feeling, I am bringing the words out. They don't frighten me anymore.

Once upon a time, you see, I lived in blindness. I could look with my eyes and, yes, there was the world around me full of people, a sky of stars and a girl in the mirror staring back blankly when I sought her. But to actually see – to distinguish the depths that was juxtaposed with what was there in my sight, I was not able to. And perhaps most girls cannot. Perhaps day after day for many girls on the earth, who don't get to learn the story of others, to wake up into the light of a brand-new day is merely to live over again the suffering of the last. They can't see that their memories of yesterday are just ashes. And, if they sift through them and don't find anything they'd like to keep – no grain of gold anywhere to be found – then they must leave them and seek new and worthier fires.

My memory used to war against me – a gas chamber to exterminate hope every waking morning. But that was in the past. Today, I open my eyes to my life: I am found. There is a choir of bright red robins, a joyful chorus of doves singing in triumph and wonder in the morning before a smiling golden sunrise of warmth and delight.

Samba drums and timbrels strike, beat notes of purple, radiant green and yellow from a distant jungle deep in my soul, and the mystic heat of having trekked through the depths of life rises out of the pores of my body. I dance. I am found and not lost. Let the day begin, the new day that thrills me to enter in.

Chapter One

Once eons ago, I was a ten-year-old child. I remember parallel bars on the playground, giggling about Andrew, Thomas – boys I thought were cute, sleepover parties, nails, shoes, and clothes.

I was ten, and I also knew serious meditation at such a young age. In flashes of consciousness depending on the wind, I would see my own gravestone, dark and real, underneath a cold, gray sky. Small yellow flowers skirted the front: I had been loved. I took this as a premonition that God would surely answer my prayer and keep those dark nights hidden. Since I'd been loved, I figured no one would ever know my secret.

"Nothing is hidden that will not be made manifest." I don't remember where I heard the saying, but it threatened me like a distant storm cloud, ominously thundering, and ever in my dreams after that. Maybe it was church – or a verse from some song, telling everyone that all things will eventually come to light. The awful, hidden truths that you wish weren't known would eventually be revealed. The words told me that, no, you won't take it to your grave, little girl. But I prayed in terror and tried to return to the playground.

On the brink of adolescence, everything was easy when I was away from home. There was a push, like I was a small bird shoved out of a high nest – that was just the way things were. I didn't have to think much socially; I made friends; I knew how to laugh; I did fine at school.

A very small taint, however, was growing. It grew in the blood that flowed through my veins. Looking back, I don't know if it was typical teenage girl fears, or the beginnings of the darkness that would engulf my consciousness for years of my life to come.

In the fourth grade, I remember coming to know the duality of existence for myself. There were two of myself, and there was no joining them back together. I was for many reasons unlike other girls. For one, I was black, and none of my friends were black. My family lived in Suwanee, in a suburban neighborhood with good schools and safe streets. In the early 90s, minorities made up what seemed like just a handful of families in the area. I knew that my family didn't have a lot of money (my parents had five children, after all), and my friends seemed to have plenty. Second, I had sexual desires that were premature, while my friends seemed innocent. They all had fathers who were present, normal, loving dads, while mine was destroying my life as often as there was opportunity. I did not know what to make of it all.

I did not know what to make of it all two years earlier when I was only eight. What does a child know at eight? My son is eight. I rock him on my lap when he is tired or sick. He knows that I am here to protect him, and we pray together before bed at night. The night doesn't have to frighten him. He is figuring out his place in the world, seeing its darkness and its light. Every moment, though, he is held in love. He is learning multiplication, facts, and he loves craft. His innocence is something to hold onto, and I want him to understand things, and to laugh, and to be comfortable. He is my firstborn, my baby.

What kind of evil goes unchecked and brings a parent to tear down the sanctity of a child's innocence, and to cross forbidden, unthinkable boundaries? I cannot and never want to imagine it. I cannot explain.

When I was eight, one evening, my father, my sister, and my little brothers were all watching T.V. in the living room. My father had let me drink some of the wine he had, and I remember feeling silly, playful. I was laughing, and he was laying on the couch under a blanket. He pulled me down onto himself, started tickling me, and got very close to my belly. He suddenly pulled me under his blanket and put his hand inside of my tights. He touched me between my legs and I, not knowing what to do or think, didn't stop him. My world froze, and the combination of alcohol and confusion kept me stuck, the world spinning, my siblings so close to me, my father – an unfamiliar stranger. I didn't speak and I didn't know what would happen next, my eight-year-old mind both shocked and numbed at once.

That night, before I went to bed, my father came and whispered to me that I could never tell my mom about how we "played." Because if I did, someone would be killed. I didn't know what he meant by that; maybe it was me that would be hurt, maybe it was my mom, maybe it was him. In my mind, I didn't want any of those scenarios, so I kept quiet and didn't tell. I had night and daydreams from that moment forward. They were full of tickling and of death. All the colors of the universe as I'd known it and hoped it to be swirled together into one lump of murky darkness. Nothing was clear. I was blind.

Because, like so many mothers, mine worked a lot, there were plenty of opportunities after that first night for my father to molest me. Sometimes he would find me alone in the room I shared with my sister and take advantage of me there. Sometimes it would happen on the same couch in the living room. Sometimes he would pull me into his bedroom. He became bolder and moved from touching, to pushing himself against me, to putting his mouth on my body. I was not always afraid, but I hated the confusion. I didn't know why this was happening or what I could do about it. I would sometimes try to hide, or to push him away, but he always won. I was too small and too confused to do anything but accept that this was my life at home. This continued in darkness for the next five and a half years.

Chapter Two

I was the only person on the planet in my real life, where all things were plain and naked under the sun. The rest of the universe was light years away, all others together with one another, logically, sensibly, happily. But my reality was a blur. My days and years were being sucked into a frightening vacuum, disappearing into nothing. I was a little girl, but I began to think I might surely die before I could make sense of my life and finally find myself in the mess of it all. No one saw me.

Except my father.

Gradually, my eyes came to see every adult man as a predator. Each one of them, a pastor, a teacher, a trusted family friend, a neighbor, was suspiciously likely, in my mind, to be hiding his true nature until wiser eyes were closed. They were not necessarily evil, because I didn't yet understand that what was going on was indeed evil. But somehow every black man, like my father, was someone who would take advantage of a child, who saw me as a sexual object and couldn't be trusted to be alone with.

We would go to church, and if there was a man who even slightly resembled my father in any way, I imagined that he would no doubt try to rape me if he ever got me alone. Because my own father was active in the church, I came to associate church with deception. The singing and reading of holy verses meant, from what I could see, nothing to them – but how was it that no one else could tell? What would these praying, shouting, preaching people do within the walls of their own homes, when no eyes were watching? Were they any different from my father, who slithered through darkness?

The things I did not know, I came to learn. This dual existence I maintained was not wholly normal, not wholly acceptable. With this knowledge, my insecurities grew. What would others think of my truth? What was I besides an object – a broken one at that? Was He real, or just a myth, behind which any deceptive clergyman could hide and carry out his unspeakable aims? Was God truly in control, or did we all roam around on this globe, lucky or unlucky, at the hands of chance? At twelve, thirteen years old, I could not see myself beyond those years. I did not imagine that I could bear to know the answers to all my questions.

How could a young girl hold so much inside – a pit deep, cyclonic, black, and savagely hopeless?

Chapter Three

At twelve, I was virtually dead beyond my senses. Of course, I could walk, and talk, and pretend to be normal when I needed to. But the hole inside was powerfully destructive, and all my life had fallen in. Like many girls (especially at a time when social media did not exist), I wrote in diaries to gather the thoughts that were scrambling about like flies over a carcass.

I wanted so badly to articulate what was happening to me. I wanted to write out questions for God – prayers to Him, if I could only believe He was there. I wanted to write about the disgust I was accumulating for myself like dirt filling a grave, for not knowing how to stop the abuse that had already rotted my life.

Are there words for such guilt? Are there words for such sadness? Is there a word for a blackness so permeating?

I wanted to write, but I found tears each time I tried. Tears of hopelessness, of embarrassment, of frustration would wet my trembling hands, and there was no space to fathom the words. So, I wrote about whatever else I could.

For a while, at least a year or so, my diary entries centered on a lump that was growing in my left breast, which I was sure was cancer. I hadn't told anyone, because I was afraid that I was quickly dying – it was so large. To tell my mom would be to burden her, was already so busy. I wondered how my dad hadn't known, for how often he had touched me. I assumed he didn't care or didn't want to deal with it. As for me, already feeling like walking death, so numb and withdrawn, I didn't know if I was worth the trouble of stopping whatever was to come. I had only lived a handful of years, and they had been covered with so severe a night that I saw life as useless.

I was like a bird who had been stricken blind and fallen from the sky immediately after finding flight. Like a flightless, useless bird that would now pass on back into the obscure earth, no one to affect, no one to notice me.

I remember writing in those diaries about my fear of anyone knowing about the lump. I tried as much as my barely existent faith could to pray it away. But, deep in my heart, I wanted to let it just consume me because my life had so little meaning. However, I did care about my younger siblings, and the thought of not being around to help look after them frightened me. They would be left, without me, in the hands of people who couldn't be trusted. What if my father got to them one day when I wasn't around? What if they eventually came to suffer the same dark fate that had emptied my soul?

I was scared, but I needed to tell my mother. I scraped up a small amount of courage, and one morning before she went to work, I told her that I had breast cancer. Not fully understanding that children my age were very unlikely to develop breast cancer, I was put at ease when she said it was probably just a benign cyst. I went to the pediatrician that same week, was scheduled for a biopsy soon after, and was relieved to know that my mom was right: it was not cancer. All my twelve-year-old forebodings about death had come to nothing, and I was allowed to remain alive. Perhaps my life had a purpose, and the broken bird wouldn't yet know dust to dust.

What the whole cancer-scare experience did at a young age was give me at that young age a break from my father. I was bandaged across my chest and had missed a lot of school, so I needed my body to heal and to return to normal. I think he saw this and kept away from me. There were a few times when he would attempt to get me alone, or to try to touch me in slight ways after my surgery. But, little by little, I realized that the worst of the molestation had come to an end...physically at least.

Chapter Four

When I started high school a few months later, I was overwhelmed by the urge to be at once both seen and unseen. I wanted to be beautiful – for people to accept and like me, while never getting to truly know me. I didn't have anything else. I did not know who in God's name I was or could possibly become.

My social life was odd. It was a strange mixture of friends, some with whom I connected because they, too, were tragically shy, and others with whom I'd found a way to play the game, managing to seem normal and fit in. And so not knowing, what to make of anything, wanting to feel a part of something tangible, I obsessed over my hair, my makeup, and my clothes. I learned to sew a weave with the ten-dollar package of human hair from the beauty supply store, which was all-important. I could make my hair look like I got it done every week, and I felt pretty. Dollar store makeup pencils, mascaras, glitters, all decorated my face until I looked like a much older teenager. And this attracted boys, left and right.

At school, I could find comfort in the fact that I was noticed – at least physically – and wanted. I could fit in and look normal. The attention I would get was a distraction from the nothingness, the consuming darkness of confusion that had slowly crushed me to numbness and hollowed out my soul.

Dangerously concerned about my appearance, I became fascinated with the power I had over food and over my body. I developed an eating disorder. There would be long stretches of days on which I ate very little: broccoli or some cookies at lunch, and maybe a small bite of something insubstantial later. And then there were days when I ate nothing. Not one single thing for a day – in an attempt to earn a respectable discipline and to have a grip over my soul.

Sometimes I would challenge myself to eat only after some random late hour, like 4:00, and then only a candy bar to keep me from fainting. But the problem came when I would eat entire boxes of snacks, or too much of anything that was good. I would feel like I had fallen into a hole, like I had lost all control over the one thing that made me feel strong.

I would stick two fingers to the back of my tongue and vomit it all out into the toilet when I was done. Doing this was my way of making sure I remained thin, and that I could manage something in an otherwise unmanageable world. It was like this off and on for the next seven years of my life. Another secret to cloak my reality.

Just now, as I reflect, I see how the pieces were made to fit in that strange puzzle of years. Without the distractions, without my preoccupation with shallow social acceptance, what would those times have done to me? Surely, I would have become part of the dust, wandering through deserts of obscurity until they covered me – my eyes burned out by pain.

The irony of having had my own "cancer" scare right before entering high school is that only a couple of years later, my father would have his own. One morning, as he was upstairs in his bathroom, I heard a loud crashing noise. It was him. He had fallen to the floor during a massive seizure. This had never happened before, and after being taken to the hospital, my family learned that he had a brain tumor that was cancerous and life-threatening. He would need surgery, thus beginning a series of treatments and memories gauzed over in a blur. What to think, what to feel?

My father's illness, of course, took its toll on our immediate and extended family. He couldn't work, and there was an air of pity surrounding him that I couldn't even pretend to absorb. Months passed rapidly, full of hospital visits and a confusing ever-presence that made me want to flee for all reasons. I don't remember thinking about many things except flight. We just existed in that sad, odd state for months, as if our breath was being held, until the thin ice on which our foundations lay was cracked open. And all things upon it fell through.

Chapter five

It was toward the middle of my sophomore year in high school when I decided to break the silence that had wrapped my secret and tormented me with shame and anguish for years. I didn't want to tell anyone because I was immensely embarrassed by this weight, this unspeakably dark stigma I had borne for so long. And, above all now, I was very afraid to hurt my mother. It would bring her so much difficulty, and there was so infinitely so much at stake. She had five children, and I was the oldest. It would affect everyone. But that is why I had to speak: their safety – all of our safety – was in jeopardy.

During a conversation in our room one day, I had discovered that what had happened to me, had also happened, and may have still been happening to my sister. My sick father, despite his cancer treatments and his physical weakness, was no less capable of monstrosities. My heart sank into the pit of my body, and I had no more time or options left. I had to talk, and this was real; my life and all of our lives would change and had to change.

I gathered the dust that remained of my lost voice the next day and told my mother that we needed to go somewhere and talk. There are no words for the fear I felt. She could tell something was wrong, and so we got in the car and she drove us to Kroger. When we got there, we didn't get out – just sat there, me with shaking hands and legs, a heart pounding so rapidly I might surely have died before the words came out. She asked me to speak. I looked at her, tears welling in my eyes, and forced the sounds of it out. "Daddy used to...touch me."

I was afraid of what would follow. After I had explained what had happened to me and what I suspected he may have done to my sister, after many tears, my mom, through a melting voice full of sadness and resolve, said that she would call the police and take care of things. The next moment, my cell phone rang. It was my father; I suppose he was looking for us. Maybe he had sensed something was turning in the universe. Maybe he sensed that he was about to fall from the side of the world, or that in our own ways, we all were.

I didn't answer, and I would never take the chance to speak to him again. The truth was out, and it felt worse than I imagined any death might feel.

My father was found and arrested that day, and to be honest, I don't know how long he was in jail. I don't know the details of his imprisonment, and I did not think too deeply about them. The sentence was messy because he was terminally ill, and I had only put down one burden to pick up another, more deadly oppressive.

Aunts, cousins, grandparents, essentially my entire family on my father's side, who had always been active and loving in my life, did not believe that their relative could be guilty of sexually abusing his own child. Whereas before it all came out, phone calls, visits, and outings were normal among members of our family;

after the fact, all of it immediately stopped. My mother was very protective and saw to it that communication between me and my father's family would be extremely limited.

I found out, though, that they all believed I had made up the entire story. They said that I had spoken out for the sake of attention, and that none of it was true. Their disbelief and accusations hurt deeply, and they left an everlasting scar. It did make sense, though, that there was great hesitancy on their part to accept that the brother they'd known, the son they'd raised, the uncle they'd loved, was someone guilty of horrendous sins against a family he'd always worked so hard to make appear perfect. No one could believe that he was a person who outwardly loved children but could rape his very own.

I had always had a difficult time trying to navigate the dichotomy of my identity before that time. It was necessary to be a normal person in public, and to hide the secrets of my home life. But now, with my own family accusing me of lying, this was more than I could bear. I became a walking shell. Trying to appear normal and to find pieces of happiness and hope was everything. I continued on the right track as I could with the routine of school, working to save as much money as I could, and tried to take care of my siblings to help my mom with the new responsibility of being a single parent to five children.

Inside of me, whatever structure on which I had found the nerve to try and stand was constantly falling, and I imploded into a mess of bits. My daily living was a test of sorts, an awful game of waking up, building pieces of an identity, praying desperately for so many facets of being that other people seemed to possess naturally, and hoping that what I presented to the world every day was not as dreadful as what I felt inside. Some days I could see pages of a melancholy story coming together; I could see with hope a good thing being formed of my life. Other days, though, I was blind to who I was to be, and how I was to be anything at all.

Chapter Six

I was eighteen years old in January of 2005. I had recently enrolled in a community college in Lawrenceville, Georgia, and was living in an apartment with my boyfriend. Thinking I had things figured out more than most others my age, I aimed to be ambitious and tried to chisel out a purpose for myself somewhere in the world. I worked hard at a big warehouse store, saving as much money as I could to perhaps move away to attend a bigger school, or to start my own business. I had two dreams: to become a restaurant owner, and to be a teacher; I had always loved kids.

The ideas I would get from books and from the few close friends I had at the time made risk and wonder seem like delicious ingredients to a worthy life. It was a season of unfolding, of breathing, and of carefully trying out the wings I'd just trusted myself to fly with.

Pitted against that hope, though, was a sickening and weighted terror that had taken refuge in the hollow between my heart and stomach. It had lived there dormant for all time, but as far as I could see, I had learned to manage it by turning a blind eye. My blind eyes were useful for this. After a point though, it awoke and I felt it moving until it consumed every inch of the hollow, seeming as much a part of me as my blood. It took a hold of my words and my thoughts; it drugged me. How and why such darkness was to be lived through was beyond me. "Why?" I asked.

Early one morning before I was supposed to go to work, I stopped by to visit my mom. I went up the stairs to her bedroom, and instead of finding her watching a movie or doing laundry, she was rolled up crying. I went over to her and asked what the matter was. She sat up and prepared her words. They came out, so unexpected, so hoped for, so unbelievable: "Your dad died today." And the weight of all weights eternally carried broke my knees and brought me to the ground. There were no words.

Time melts.

Three or four years filled the space between the last time I had laid eyes on my father. The years, washing me physically of his presence, still warped my mind in sheer horror. They seemed like forever – and yet – never, ever enough. The last time, besides the hundreds in my relentless nightmares, was in a hallway outside of a courtroom. He was in a wheelchair, unable to walk due to complications from cancer. Despite his pitiful appearance, fear gripped my soul at the sight of his face. I could only look down to keep from disappearing in cold fright. What more could he say? What more could he do? He had already killed me so many times over.

Before and after that day, dreams came like omens regularly. I would fall asleep and be smothered by his hand over my face, or choked to death with a long black sock, or pushed out of the back window of our house or chased down to be killed. If it were night and I was awake, walking around the house, I could almost feel eyes on me, like he was watching me through cracks in the blinds, waiting to repay me for speaking out. He still stalked my world and haunted me. For the longest time, both in my sleep and waking moments, he continued to haunt. I prayed the hand of Jesus all day long to keep him and his ghosts away.

The prospect of seeing the face of my father was mortifying. To look at the features – even the memory of those lips, wide nose, black hair – chilled my gut. This horror blended somehow with pictures in my mind of who I saw him as so long ago, before he suffocated the innocence of my eight-year-old body and my immortal soul. And so, there was horror amid sadness, instead of the satisfactory closure I'd imagined I might know when, if ever, he died. How many precious hours had I already poured into pillows with tears of shame and anger? And now on the eve of his burial, I had more. Heavy pain bore down on my heart for all things, above all, for my mother. For my brothers, too, for whom the death was also significant, laden with confusion and hurt.

When we arrived at the funeral, to bear the weight of the steps, the air, the reality of life was like trying to walk through lead. It was like trying to walk through lead. It was not right, and nothing about the world was right. I wanted to leave.

"Why should I have to see it? Why should my innocent brothers? Why should songs be sung to remind and to chill me? Why should lies be told to paint over an ugly life, one of deceit and dark things? Why should I have to accept cousins, and aunts, uncles, grandparents who somehow saw me as an adversary in this charade, when I wanted no part – not one – in any of it?" I thought.

Perhaps all of my fears had gathered here: walking into a room full of what were essentially strangers, who had passed the worst judgment on me, barely yet a woman. I did not know all of my father's family, but I did know that they saw me as less than I was, a liar, somehow responsible for a conflict I did not create. Their views, their words for me, would somehow mold my early adulthood. I would come to live as if the whole of the earth saw me as a blemish, a fault to be covered over, wiped away.

I couldn't swallow, so I sat down. I didn't want to go in. Nevertheless, the stout hand of some unknown aunt pulled me up by my wrist and then in – "Go on in there. Go on in and look at your daddy." Her words were insensitive and repulsive, but I was frozen deep inside myself. So, I went, stiffly, and sat in the area for the family, head down the entire time. One hour or many more – the horror of it all – a numbing time. To look at down at my father's body was a sin that I avoided as if it would kill me there, too.

I wonder if I had abandoned my fright for some godless reason and had seen his face, if today I would be even more haunted by these features? There are times, cold and plain and for no reason at all, that memory of one of them flashes before my eyes, as visible as my own hands are now. To bear even these reminders of his lingering presence moves me coldly, and charges me to pray. I pray for protection because I know that his shadow would still consume and kill my vulnerability if I allowed it. Years fall like rain.

Chapter Seven

The weight can grow too heavy and eventually your heart will stop. Don't carry it; don't carry it. My burden grew like some nasty, heavy, unspeakable fungus growing on stone, covering my throat, my eyes, my feet – my entire self. No matter how I tried to get it off me and leave it to starve and die alone as it should, I could not escape. I took long baths to heal the ache of living every day. I would so often sink my ears, my eyes, below the water line, under the depths of the possibilities of the water. Many times, I opened myself up to fading away and dying just like that, right there in the bath. Fade trying to be clean and not feel pain.

I managed to pray sometimes, although I did so with distrust and resentment. "Dear God, please take away my sadness. Dear God, please let my mom be happy. Dear God, please protect my siblings. Dear God, please let me know if You are there."

I attribute it now only to God, who indeed answered my scattered prayers. By then, I was gathering up shards of strength from the broken pieces of myself and managing to push through. I graduated high school and tried to become someone by going to college. In 2007, I started attending Kennesaw State University, and moved onto campus. It was a difficult transition for me because I was forcing myself into a situation in which I would have to be a person. I would have to live with strangers; I would have to try to become things I didn't know how to be. It was hard for me to speak up in classes where discussion was expected. It was hard for me to join clubs, to even so much as go to the dining hall during lunchtime because I didn't want to have eyes on me. Surely, if I myself had to work so hard to make sense of who I could possibly be, it would be a daunting task for all others. So, I feared giving anyone the opportunity.

Chapter Eight

It felt like the right thing to do: to leave this world with which my soul disagreed, to lay down the hard fight and surrender all my fears, to fade away until all that was left was the echo of an insufficient heartbeat. And then, let that fade away, too.

One afternoon, in a season more isolating that any I'd ever been through, I took a bath and let my head stay below the water longer than the few usual seconds of contemplation. The normal energy required to lift myself back up, to breathe to keep living, was nowhere to be found in my body. I lay there, looking up at a dingy beige ceiling. What if I just rested there, what if my roommates found my bloated body and I was carried away from this final place? My family, my brothers, coming to solemn goodbyes stained with confusion and disbelief.

My spirit somehow making its way to Jesus, although I had questioned and found myself disappointed with his company, having given up this life He'd lain me in. He would be welcoming, but the meeting would be lukewarm and half-lived – exactly like my life. I could not accept it. But to continue pursuing life, relief eluding me, how could I do it any longer? Little girl, no identity, no fire left, so many tears, and such a weary, heavy heart.

More than terror, more than fatigue with the impossible burdens of reconciling simultaneously with the world, God, and growing up – more than these weights kept me submerged. When I considered the possibilities of the future compared with my dreams – who I would become, what I would do – I saw so little hope. It seemed there was nothing before me except, as far as I fathomed, a sort of desert, an emptiness that could only be filled by more emptiness, a barren expanse, a drawn-out death.

So, nearly fading away in the tub, two things kept me alive that day: my family, and my anger. Did the devils that led me here deserve victory? No, no, for all the world, no. Not my destruction, so early in the fight for life. "Something," God, "to go on," I prayed. "Please give me some strength to move." I opened my eyes: no angels, nothing I could see to help. Pushing my head up through the heaviness of the water, I sat up, not sure how. But I was not dead, not dead: I would war another minute, another day.

As if my world were a ball, and the universe was a pool table, I was instantly knocked and rolled in directions almost automatically. I worked hard at side jobs, paid my bills, got myself through college with good grades. I had tried to be good, and everyone treated me so. If I were invited to a party, it was to reassure my friends that I was not for parties. I watched my language, I prayed, I prayed, I prayed. I read my bible on Saturday nights, alone. For years I tried to be as good as I could be, to do the right things as I saw them, all the while asking for wisdom in case I wasn't seeing them right.

But the hole in my chest had not shrunk, had not been filled, still hindered me, still needed love more severely, and still kept me from loving myself. I continued, most nights, to cry into whatever would hold my tears. All I had to look forward to, the progress that would see me some way out of the valley that had been my hellish home, would not come. to that would see me some way out of the hellish valley that had become my home would not come.

So, I began to wonder about my soul: was I a child of God? Was He not love? Was He listening? Why, then, did I want to die? Why was I brought into a world, where little girls are used and made to live silent, hollow lives thereafter until they crumble into dust? Why was I born with such a father – what kind of God would allow it? Why was there fear, so much fear in the air I breathed? Why, why, why? So many questions, and never an answer. Only echoes of themselves, hushed by my own feeble hopes of surviving them.

One very weighted day, I felt, at any moment, like all the grey damage of a storm would bring my head to falling clean off my neck like a swollen, heavy fruit. The same feeling I'd had in the tub not two years before, had made its way back to my soul. My mind was full and numb, and I wanted to be free.

On the threshold of breaking irreplaceably, when my mom, the one constant element of light, told me to go to the store with her. It was as if her spirit sensed the death in my own dying sun and gave it new life with her own light. And so, I went, tired but wanting to live, trying not to show what was inside, as I always had. My head beat like the footstep of doom personified and I with it in the car for 15 minutes that fall day. We arrived at the vitamin store, my mom and I, and thereby my life – who would have thought was saved.

When I entered the tiny store, I saw at the end of one aisle a swiveling rack full of greeting cards and small gifts. With no interest in vitamins, I was drawn to the watercolors on some of the cards. I flipped through, reading the quotes on each one, finding myself a little pocket of delight for a few minutes. Words always had that effect on me, but this time, a word on one of the cards brought me back from my own dying. As if the very God of all this universe – so distant until then – had made time that afternoon to finally answer my prayers, my million prayers, at once, in a few seconds, on this rack in that small shop.

I disappeared from that place for a moment to listen to the words of God, translated conveniently for my desperate sake by Rainer Maria Rilke. New life came forth from these words: "Do not seek the answers, which cannot be given to you now, because you would not be able to live them. Live the questions, and one day you will live into the answers."

And with this tiny square greeting card, the noxious cloud of confusion, and sadness, and anger, and all the questions they carried, all together dissipated, burned away by a blazing, bright new sun. With unweighted faith, I walked toward my freedom.

Chapter Nine

I am alive in about a hundred ways on this day. Dancing, laughing through the breeze; my body, mind, and spirit are here, and all are moving. Closing my eyes at any moment, I see and feel golden light beaming warmly before me, the color of love.

I am a conscious woman. My life is full of color, molded from vibrant clay, and even if I tried, I could not deny the joy. From time to time, as I'm caught in the world's rhythms of movement and forgetting, it's as if God reaches down His mighty hand, takes His forefinger, and bursts the little bubble I'd allowed to form over myself. My heart laughs at the spectacle of my imaginations: all the self-pity, the stress, the longings I chose to focus on to my own detriment. My heart laughs to breaking, while cold tears stream down from my eyes and refresh my sight.

I see what I had temporarily forgotten: the intimacy of God's mercy. Fistfuls of prayers from years of anguish now fall through my fingers like fine, worn sand, falling through time. I have had needs that my life depended on, my children's lives, and when there wasn't a reason to hope logically, God answered my prayers. I never deserved it, and I still don't. Yet the rays of golden yellow light still shine in quiet moments across my face, and I look up and fall to my knees. With the weight of gratitude overpowering my senses, I fall to my knees. I know that if my secrets had indeed remained hidden, and if I had gone, as I so often contemplated, to an early grave, or had simply lived in silence among fears and horrors, I know that the golden joy I carry would never have been conceived, even in my most audacious dreams.

Human beings are created from the dust of the earth. We are organic and therefore, like all living growing things, are affected in intricate ways by the environment. No two of us are the same when it comes down to how the nutrients in our soil affect us, how the temperature of the breeze impacts our ability to thrive. We are all more like plants than robots – unpredictable, with formulas for how to survive, yes – dirt, water, sunlight – but then all impacted so differently by the variables of living this life.

Take a shell of a girl, whose body's been ravaged and hollowed, self-worth gutted by rape, mind blown away like puffs of a body's ashes. Living hurts, and so to heal the pain, there's death directly, or there are things to take that lead more slowly but also directly to the same death. Or, there is patience and discipline, waiting for God to answer your prayers and, hopefully, you can wait that long.

Take a person, any person, addicted, hurt, angry, hurt, sad...hurt. This thing we call time that we rely on is not, contrary to popular belief, the thing that heals. Time in a hospital, time in rehab, time in bed to sleep it off – time in denial to ignore it away – no, time is no healer. It's a vacuum, a space of prolonging, a thing that waits on other things before work is done.

What heals is the truth: uncovered, spoken, complete,

truth. Asking for his help, God showed it to me. The truth, which He always speaks, was that I could not fathom the answers to my numberless questions; they were not for me to know, because I am not God. This is what He spoke:

> *Silly girl, the truth is, you are not alone. I am here, and, yes, in your eyes it seems awful but, in fact, all of it is bearable and all for a purpose so magnificent you can't believe. The truth is, I built you for this. You will bring light to dark places, as I brought light after yours.*

What are you running from? What dirt have you heaped upon the words of truth that are written in the ground in front of your very feet? I ask you to bend down and allow yourself to fall on your knees. Brush the words clean and ask your God to help you interpret the difficulty. This is now your plot, the land of your truth. Carry it with you, scoop it into your hands, eat it, if you must, in order to keep it. Just don't walk away from it: in truth, you cannot.

Somehow seeing ourselves and our truth, we see it in this world too. Look around and decipher what really is there: who you are in the midst of these mirages, what you are here for on the sands beneath them. You, like everyone, are uniquely fashioned, and your thoughts, emotions, memories – your very breath – are all special. And, if you see the truth in what you can give to others by planting yourself firmly in the soil of it, your fruit may nourish generations to come with an abundance only God's orchestration could yield.

When you think of where to go from here, what I can share with you is this. Do not call yourself by any label that robs you of your present or future glory. You are not a victim. No, such a word is for a one-dimensional process, and it overlooks the intricate weaving taking place in the new creation you are becoming. What good has the word "victim" ever done for anyone who is called by it? The connotation is one of defeat and pity; but, glory to God, your life overcomes. Beautiful and precious girl, you overcome! You have been subjected to evil, and shaped by its lessons, but you have always been and are destined to be so much more than its victim.

And, secondly, since you are not a typical or shallow being, know and walk in what you, in fact, are. Look at you, child of God...breathing His air, heart beating with His blood. You must be light, and love, and life, as are all creations that are His. If you don't take hold of this understanding, by default the world is given that charge. The world's understanding is unsteady, ever-changing, never sufficient. It tells, like the most devious friend, lies so sweetly promising one relief after another, forever until death, if you just obey.

It is exactly what Eve told God in the Garden of Eden; "*The serpent beguiled me, and I did eat.*" Society has its way of telling us who to be, and what we must do in order to find fulfillment. But we must have eyes that see and understand, that perceive the deception of empty things that beckon to us. You live, and you will continue to learn. There will be angels sent, as there have been before, to guide you towards the glory you were brought here to manifest.

I also pray for the wisdom to know what to make of the ashes that remain, and I am still searching for wisdom, for answers. Listen. There is a voice inside of you and it's not your heart, it's not your conscience, and it's not easy to distinguish from other voices without some discipline. It's as if your child was in a choir – and you know which one, after listening, is yours. No matter the primary confusion or the proximity of the pitches, you know your own. It's the same concept that you have to apply – listening to the voice that is from Heaven. It's that voice that tells you what to do, and how to mine the treasures held in each hour of your life. They are only found when you dig into the depths of who you are: mind, body, heart, soul, and take what is there at the end of yourself.

This is important because time is at stake. Go down into yourself only a bit, and there are goods to serve only your body, for only a while. A little further, your heart, which has to be – this I do know – left to be dealt with by God Himself. Deeper down still, is your mind, which changes with the wind and so is unreliable. And, finally, your soul, which you can only get to after going through the rest. Yes, go down into it; get to know the colors that are there, the sights and sounds, the urges. This is what is warred after. This is where your treasure lies, which God placed inside of you. You were brought here to bear it for the world.

Memory is a superpower full of potential – dangerous potential – if we are unaware of its might. I now find it easy to forget the details of the days of the life I once had. It happened by accident when I prayed for sadness and shame to leave me, and they did, and now I forget. I forget that I was ever young, that I ever had such a secret to bear. I forget that I ever had a father, such a one to fear and to hate as the one who was there with me. The times were real enough, but, maybe for the sculptor, for the poet, for the artist working through their medium to communicate their reality, it can be replaced in those pieces of translation. If I compose a sad song, it could seem that particles of my sadness become the song instead of themselves. I become powerful in that sense; indeed, any artist is a person of power because they create and thus alter reality.

    There is no sense now in feeling sorry for myself. I don't allow myself to make a lifestyle out of excuses, although they get by at times when I'm overwhelmed or frustrated. A few tears, several groaned prayers, and silence, and the weight is lifted under new-found strength. The Lord reminds me that I don't have to understand any of it, that I don't have to enjoy it or feel powerful throughout the hours of the days with which He's blessed me anew. I unfold memories of His kind mercies, so undeserved and unforeseen, from their corners of my truth and spread them out, letting the air of this entire weight filter through what's been before and what shall continue to be. To God be all the glory, I lift my head and onward can proceed.

    What is an excuse when we test it? Some cuff to hold us, linked ever yet to the past full of its defeats and grueling trials. An excuse is a tool of self-degradation; to say why a pain is intolerable for me to bear, to say why a task is beyond my ability, to allow the winds of change and growth to blow over me and to refuse to run with them, as if the small fistful of self-pity I retain for myself counts for anything at all – is fruitless. I have found that accepting excuses from myself has never brought anything but regret. I have found myself, many times over, looking at the same test that has already been presented, and I realize that I was not meant to run from it with all my reasons for remaining weak. The self-pity we hold on to is no substitute for the love of God, whose grace and mercy run abundant and full, never leading us to dead-end or barren valleys.

Every morning, the birds bring their songs to the world anew; perhaps they are thankful for yet another day, their wings still crisp and poised to fly, the sky still clear and waiting to be soared through. I want to be like these birds, praising the Lord in the hush of a sleeping world.

In the quiet of the dawn, I can't outdo myself and can't be outdone by the noise or commotion of the bustling day. I take a few moments to be alone, with more of God to myself, with all of me to dance and sing and fly for Him.

One Sunday morning, on an early walk, I stepped over a couple of crushed plastic liquor bottles and a few pieces of what looked like drug debris. Imagining that some of the many homeless people I'd seen the nearby intersection had spent their night fighting hard habits, I wondered. How was it that I escaped that fate? How had I not spent even a night on a street bench, behind a store, under some outdoor shelter? I had, after all, fought many battles – not a single one with the strength to win – but somehow was not thrust into the life so many others had found themselves in, on this very street, only the night before.

Who was I to step over their remains and not consider? And it came to me, a miracle long past but newly discovered, like the bone of a dinosaur right there on the sidewalk, like the story of the footprints, where the man who thought he had trodden his most dangerous paths alone, did not realize he had been carried all along. I wasn't ever waiting for Him to come, not ever waiting for Him to answer my cries.

He was always there, carrying me.

I think if you look around you – really take a silent, focused breath of moments and look around you – there is, floating about through spaces in the air like drifting feathers, everything that you need. Looking up at the moon on a dark and quiet night, I found that I am both small and large, great enough to remain on the face of this planet and continue the work of my hands, but not as significant as the trees, or the celestial bodies above and around me.

I opened a book that taught me that I am and must continue to be a warrior. I spoke to a friend and was given the love I had sought during such long and lonesome months. I knelt to be touched, and the hand of God breathed life into my dying soul and showed me that I am never without. Every time the darkness clouds about me, and it does ever so often, I am reminded to breathe the air and all its truths all around me. There is something of a veil, a blindness that threatens to plant itself without breathing this in. It is important and possible to acknowledge that there are two ways of seeing yourself in the world, but only one of them is the truth. You are a child of God, of the light and not of darkness. It all comes together if you let go and hold on, hold on and let go.

I am a child of God. I am held, called according to His purpose, and precious in His sight. I will live my days now in exploration of the wilderness of this path. In exploring, there is a search for a treasure, something novel and worthy to be sought. You have to remove yourself from the mundane every day in order to seek it out, because, by definition, it lies hidden from the well-trodden path.

Women have to open their minds to change and to fear. These are essentials for growing and finding new ways of leading the life you've been given. We can do this by reading, we can do this through travel, and we can open ourselves up to it by pushing ourselves into unfamiliar territories. Learning a new skill, becoming acquainted with unknown circles, moving into different and unexpected surroundings, all of these are explorations in a sense. They not only startle you out of the gray dust that sometimes settles over living for all of us. They also open the pores of your senses, infusing fresh oxygen to the breathless regions, gifting creativity and joy, fulfillment and rest.

Even as I write this, I know that another treasure calls to me from some exotic place, and a new adventure is needed, and is approaching. I am a mother and a teacher, a friend and a daughter, a sister and an artist in my own right, and a woman – like so many others – with gifts yet untapped and fruits whose seeds I have not sown. I know that it's for me to bring my dreams into being, even those dreams that are still a colorful, hazy blur in the distance. I know because I feel God speaking to me in the depths of my heart that I have been given these days to make real the things He's given me. And so, I must venture, and learn, and speak, and create, and read, and listen, and grow, and fly.

The weights I may have carried yesterday won't suit my journey now. So, I not only leave them behind, I burn the path that leads back to them. They are parts of adventures that have already been lived: their treasures have long been found and carried away. I mount up with wings as an eagle, in fullness and without fear.

www.ingramcontent.com/pod-product-compliance
Lightning Source LLC
Chambersburg PA
CBHW030917080526
44589CB00010B/344